Copyright © 2012 by Lois M. Breit
Revised © 2017
ISBN: 978-1544726441
Cover by Pamela Beaudry

Scripture quotations are from the New International Version (NIV), New Living Translation (NLT), and the Message (MSG)

Printed in the United States of America

Single Mom Ministry

Church Leadership Guidebook

TABLE OF CONTENTS

Page

Introduction

Why Focus on Single Mothers

Current statistics indicate 35% of all U.S. families are now led by a single parent. These statistics are from the 2010 census and numbers have risen considerable. Most cities I've ministered in were comprised of 40-47% single parent homes. These single moms are often hopeless, depressed, exhausted, and desperate enough to turn to the church for help. The Church family can provide the love, hope, and forgiveness they seek along with the goals and vision they are lacking.

As Christians, we have a responsibility to be the best-equipped, intentionally-focused, and most caring resource available to those seeking both physical and spiritual help. (the vast majority of single parents attend no church)

To evangelize the next generation and offer hope to today's families, the Church must be aware of this growing demographic and adjust its ministry focus accordingly.

This means developing practical methods of ministry to single moms, incorporating curriculum and devotionals that are relevant to nearly half of the families in any given community, and establishing targeted Bibles studies and outreaches which speak to their needs.

Desiring to bring this sad statistic down is an admirable goal; however, ignoring its reality will mean more children being raised without a Christian foundation built on love, hope, forgiveness, trust, and promise.

Questions for your ministry staff

How many single mothers are in your congregation?

How many are in your neighborhood and community?

Do you know how to find the single parent demographic of your community?

What can *your* church body do to influence the life of a single mother and her children?

Do you promote relevant speakers and events in places single moms will see them (ie: laundromats, daycare centers, and apartments that have given permission)?

SINGLE MOM PERCEPTIONS

World's Perceptions

Single parents are accepted for who they are at schools, activities, bars, or their workplace. They aren't asked personal or awkward questions such as: "What happened? Why didn't you get married? Why did you get divorced?" They are not judged by the world around them, but neither are they challenged to mature, become more responsible, or see their full potential.

Church's Perceptions

Single parent families are often viewed as undisciplined, emotional and high maintenance. They can be seen as families to avoid rather than become involved with on a *friendship* level (unless they are a project or cause). Single moms often receive judgment before acceptance, correction before love, and scriptures before a relationship with God. The church often looks for a quick fix, rather than a long-term, loving, and restorative process.

Single moms with a Christian background can be treated even more harshly, because their 'sin' can't be condoned. Critical looks, harsh words, or condemnation only increase their guilt and shame, driving them further away from the place and people they need most.

Single Mother's Perception

Except for the rare few that have chosen to be a single parent, it is not a desired lifestyle. Single mothers are overwhelmed with responsibilities, financial difficulties, schedule pressures, low self-esteem, loneliness, resentment, anger, frustration, and many lack parenting skills and job training. They want to be loved and accepted, find peace of mind, and have help in raising their children. However, they often believe that none of this is possible for them because they live in an existence of hopelessness.

SINGLE MOM EMOTIONS

This is a generalized description of single mothers seeking help. There are many mothers who have walked the road of healing and restoration, while others have chosen single motherhood as a lifestyle (adoption as a single, etc). *But those seeking the help a church will often have the following view of themselves and the world around them.*

Common emotional struggles

- Hopelessness: Desperate, lonely, empty, 'dead' inside.
- Abandonment: This feeds the belief they are without value, or unlovable.
- Mental and emotional stress: Makes daily life a major chore.
- Family tensions: They can receive more criticism than encouragement, especially when forced to live with extended family that tire of their drama.
- Lacking confidence: This results in low self-esteem and a belief they cannot make sound choices, advance their education, or better their lifestyle.
- Lacking vision or goals: Directionless, just existing.
- Self condemning: Placing blame on themselves stops forward motion and healing.
- Feeling stuck: Believing they cannot change their life, their finances, their rebellious children, or themselves.
- Feeling life is out of control: Fears, anger, finances, frustrations, child/work stress.
- Weariness: Responsibilities and work load wear down the mind and body.
- Lacking trust: Because betrayal has broken their most intimate trust, they are not easily open to trusting again. Trust needs to be nurtured and earned by words, actions and example. Trusting God is just as difficult as trusting people.

These emotions are often the driving force behind more poor decisions and reactions.

Christian single moms can have these added emotional struggles

- Feelings of failure: Feeling judged and criticized as a poor mother or failed spouse.
- Feelings of being a "Bad Christian": Because her marriage failed, lacked faith, etc.
- Faith is challenged: Why did God let her down? Did she somehow let God down?
- Guilt: For past choices, or lifestyles (struggle with forgiving herself as well as others). Their self, or other imposed condemnation is a roadblock to forgiveness.
- Feelings of being an outsider in the church: Lack of acceptance into group activities, too often excluded from personal friendships.

Dangers of this mental and emotional pattern

- Suicidal thoughts and tendencies
- Vulnerability: They can become isolated. A church that doesn't understand or know how to help can drive the single parent away and into more **bad relationship choices**. They will seek love and acceptance wherever they may find it, sometimes ignoring the cost. *We don't think clearly when we are 'starving'! Esau sold his birthright for a bowl of stew when he felt he was starving; foolish choices are made when we are tired, alone, and desperate.*
- Stagnation: Without goals, there will be no change, growth, healing or health.
- Lost generation: The children will raise themselves in anger, resentment, grief, and hopelessness – living out the statistics set before them of crime, violence, promiscuity, and failures.

Importance of understanding these emotions

If the church desires to help her, it's important to understand how a single mother is emotionally feeling and how she views herself. Her feelings are real; some are justified, some are self-imposed, while others have been projected upon her. When single moms **feel they have value**, their behaviors change; when they **feel loved**, they have reason to change; when they have **good friends,** they receive sound advice that will help them to change.

Once they understand God loves them, right where they're at, that the church cares about them and their children, and that God's Word holds promises for a positive and happy future, **they find hope!** Proverbs 13:12 "**Hope deferred** makes the heart sick, but a longing fulfilled is a tree of life."

A loving, patient, understanding church body can bring life to a dying single parent family.

Now is the time, for the church to take on the challenge that society has brought them, ***embracing single parent families and giving them hope through Jesus Christ!***

A safe place to belong, to be nurtured, healed and trained.

1. She first needs to be given

- Hope
- Vision
- Life
- Encouragement
- Acceptance - friendship

2. THEN SHE NEEDS

- Training
- Education
- Discipleship
- Biblical techniques for parenting, self discipline, and decision making

SHE NEEDS FRIENDS

Psalm 68: 5-6 *"A father to the fatherless, a defender of widows, is God in his holy dwelling. God sets the lonely in families ..."*

The church can be the 'family' where single parents can feel safe.

God desires to protect and defend the 'widows' (the single mother) and her children.

Philippians 12:13 *.... But one thing I do: Forgetting what is behind and straining toward what is ahead, I press on toward the goal to win the prize for which God has called me heavenward in Christ Jesus.*

Single moms MUST let go of their past before they can embrace the future God has for them! This will take time and strong, healthy friendships, along with a relationship with Jesus, to accomplish.

SINGLE MOM PRACTICAL MINISTRY

Offer acceptance

As a single parent feels safe, she will begin to face personal issues. Love and acceptance gives her the courage to go on and meet the challenges each day brings her.

Meet immediate physical needs

Asking non-invasive questions is often what it takes to discover the needs of someone struggling alone. The need could be food, shelter, a ride, or protection from an abusive spouse. A person's mind and spirit will be open to the Word once you help alleviate their greatest source of fear or worry. It's a simple task for the church to know where the nearest women's shelters are located, have food or vouchers available, and volunteers to offer rides.

Emulate forgiveness
The church is responsible to be the example of forgiveness. Have practical teachings on forgiveness. This is foundational for the single mom's (and their children's) relationship with God, as well as any future personal relationships. They must understand forgiveness does not mean what an offender did was 'ok', that they must be the offender's friend, or that they're letting the offender off the hook. **Forgiveness means their behaviors and reactions are no longer controlled by the words and actions of someone else. They are no longer under another person's control in their lifestyle or habits**.

Forgiveness is *the key* component to healing and wholeness. If the single parent avoids this step, he or she will change very little. Here are a few indicators of a single parents' progress:
- Have they accepted God's forgiveness for themselves?
- Do they blame others or God while rarely taking responsibility?
- Will they pray with you to forgive the person who has offended them?
- Does their attitude toward the offender(s) or situation change?

Forgiveness is a choice. I've seen lives changed and families transformed when they've not only heard and experienced forgiveness, but have applied it in their lives. I've also seen women refuse to let go of their hurt and anger. They hug it like a warm blanket and cling to it like a life preserver. Ultimately, their attitude of anger and bitterness drives away their friends and family, and too often is passed on to their children.

Remember Leaders: Everyone won't be a success story, but everyone deserves to hear they can be set free from the controlling torment of an unforgiving heart!

Provide counseling

- Males should <u>**never counsel single mothers alone.**</u> Because these women have no one encouraging them, *kindness is often interpreted as fondness.*
- Do not let them become dependent upon you for their decisions or life.
- Help them evaluate how their choices cause their personal or financial crises.
- Realize suicidal thoughts can capture the mind of an overwhelmed single parent. Check out www.mayoclinic.com and search depression symptoms, to recognize the danger signs.
- Set small personal goals for them to achieve. If they consistently refuse to take action with these goals, discontinue counseling until they come back ready to make changes. You will waste your time if they are not willing to do the necessary work.

Rebuild self-esteem

Court appearances, accusations, and threats leave single mothers lacking confidence. What can the church do? **Compliment them**. Find the single parent's strengths and encourage them. Avoid unrealistic expectations. A mini spa, fresh hair-cut, manicure, or a make-up party can help heal a crushed spirit and rebuild self-confidence.

Small group involvement

Bible study or care groups are essential to understanding and having a personal knowledge of the single mom's real needs. Small groups are a training ground for trust, friendships, and lifelong behavior patterns. Groups which include couples can set a healthy example for relationships and be a good mentoring resource.

Spiritual growth

Set mini-goals for the single parent, provide a printed list of God's promises, encourage their presence in Sunday School, Bible studies, etc. Have people invest in and mentor your single parents. Older men and women can answer spiritual questions, challenge their faith, and keep them accountable for their actions.

Practical needs

Establish volunteers (or supply a list of honest local merchants, reasonably priced) to do minor car repairs, oil changes, and minor plumbing or mechanical repairs in their home. Many women do not have the strength to simply loosen bolts. Men volunteering for these jobs should always have another family member or friend accompany them to avoid idle talk or possible emotional attachments. Use wisdom.

Social life

Encourage your congregation to invite a single parent to personal gatherings, not just church functions. Divorce, death, and moves cause many to lose their friends, family, and homes. They feel they are on the outside but have a great desire to be included. Bringing a single-parent family into your social realm involves wisdom and boundaries. Single mothers can become clingy in their need, dependent in their weakness, and pesky in their loneliness. When the pastor, leadership, and congregation set guidelines and boundaries for this ministry, problems should be limited and healthy friendships can develop.

Basic guidelines:

- Limit the number of calls you take; don't let them become excessive.
- Listen to their problem, but do not let them wallow in it or continuously blame others for situations they need to control.
- Insist upon control and discipline of their children in your home (kindly, but firmly).
- Be honest with them. If they are crossing boundaries, just tell them. Truth is easier to take than wondering why they were 'cut off' or are being ignored. If they choose not to change their behaviors, let them know you cannot continue in the friendship because (the reason). Be truthful, so they can learn where they must change.
- Do not expect overnight changes in attitude or behavior. Give them time to build trust, find hope and *then* put into action better behaviors.

Too many excuses for too long a period usually means someone is not being truthful in their story or they do not really want to change. You will need discernment and must follow your instincts. Do not stay involved if you feel threatened, used or ignored. You can help someone without becoming their best friend, but you can still be friendly.

Groceries are a basic need for most single moms . . .

The church I'd wandered into brought me groceries the day my husband left. It meant so much to us that I still have the picture of that momentous gesture of love. (The picture quality is poor, but the significance of a full cupboard says it all.)

Financial planning

Financial classes are a benefit for everyone but are a necessity for single parents.

- Assess current needs and how the church can help; **always start with the immediate need and be practical.**
- Set up financial-planning classes which include:
  - ✦ Design of an actual budget with the single parent.
  - ✦ Teach tithing and giving principles, and the blessings that ensue.
  - ✦ Teach ways of establishing good credit, which will help them in renting, jobs and loans.
- Check with your local banks - some offer special programs to help single moms.
- Help *them* solve their problems, rather than take a role as their problem solver.

Sound financial decisions build character, vision, and a future. Your church can launch a single-parent family into financial stability.

Parenting classes which include discipline, order and goal setting

- Establish a parenting class taught by a couple (or single mom) that has developed practical parenting skills, raised children that are respected teens or adults, and who are respectful of others.
- Teach basic parenting techniques of discipline. We have a generation of parents who have raised themselves and do not have a basic understanding of how to parent, rather than be a buddy or emotional partner with their child.
- Teach self-discipline as well as child-discipline. We must control our behavior before we can expect to control our child's.
- Teach realistic responsibilities and difficulties that are part of parenthood. We won't always be liked for our decisions, but we must make the 'hard' parental decisions that have long-term benefits to the child.
- Include a class where a teen or young adult discusses the role their parent played in their choices and maturation process.
- Dissuade guilt. Parents blame themselves when their children make bad choices. Sometimes we've made mistakes and must forgive ourselves and seek our child's forgiveness. Other times, we have taught them wisely, but they have chosen foolishly.
- Realize it takes time and patience to change parenting techniques.

Understanding

Patience and grace will be needed as you minister to the children. In the first severa, *years* after a divorce or death, their lives are raw. Divorced parents often bicker and put their children in the middle. Some children cry because they do not see the absent parent, others cry because they have to. Some children are angry that they cannot live with the other parent while others are angry they have to talk to them. Others wait for a phone call or visit that will *never* come.

Reaching the Children

- Pray for the children: For continued prayer covering - select leadership teams, mentor families, and people who truly care about children. They may or may not interact with the family they are praying for, but continued intercession will strengthen their chances for healing and spiritual growth.
- Choose proven men in the church to encourage the boys. A grandparent couple can invest time in the life of a young girl. Just because someone volunteers, does not mean they are the person for the job. Pray about who you match up, **the wrong personal match can be more devastating than providing no one** in this role. Make sure a complete background screening has been done. Choose only those with a good reputation and consider team outings rather than one-on-one.
- Love them into wanting to behave in church, rather than expecting them to. They are grieving the loss of a parent, family, and maybe a lifestyle they once had.
- Understand that concentration, discipline, and a will to succeed in their studies can be weak for those grieving, angry, or feeling lost and left out. An older student in your church could be a good choice to tutor them in their studies. Church youth can often help these children/youth integrate into a new school as well.
- Find ways to build them up. Focus on their strengths.

Develop strong children and youth programs in the church

This is the place children are taught God's promises!

These promises help alleviate their fears, bring peace, instill joy, reveal God's plan for families and for them personally. They will learn to give, serve, help others and not just focus on their own problems.

Be aware and wise with special events:

- Father/daughter and father/son events tend to alienate children living without their absent parent.
- Don't eliminate, but expand these activities to be more inclusive. Welcome them to invite an uncle, older brother, grandparent or mentor from the church.
- Be creative. Even while emphasizing the importance of a father, mention the fact that many have significant family members (or friends) that are excited to be part of their lives and these special events.

REACH THE MOMS through Youth and Children's programs

- Personally, by phone or in person, invite the moms to all events, be sure they do not sit alone when they come to an event or church service! Engage them in conversations, beyond 'hello, I'm glad you're here'.
- Host a' meet the family' every Fall to introduce them to the church staff

Children's Programs

Develop an understanding of foundational Biblical truths, provide caring adults, and encourage spiritual and personal growth.

Youth Mission Trips

Generate a love for mankind, even when the world has not been fair to them. It helps teens focus on others, not just self.

TEAM NEEDS & VISION

Develop a team

You cannot do this ministry alone.

This ministry takes a lot of time and energy because you are working with desperate, hurting, and often unchurched/unsaved women. Avoid burnout with a strong team.

Team: Your start-up goal should be a minimum team of 4, including yourself

This team should grow as your group grows.

- **Prayer support** - Enlist an intercessor to pray for the team, moms and kids.
- **Co-leaders:** Have two people working with you. This will lighten the burden of preparation, presentation, calls, and also avoid burnout.
    - (1) Help with lesson plans
    - (2) Help with mentoring
- **Childcare Leader:** Someone (2 people lighten this load as well) to recruit and supervise childcare providers (look for church volunteers - this is a mission field and can be promoted as such when seeking qualified volunteers). This person can organize meals for the kids, and programs/crafts/studies for the children.

NOTE: I've included meals because the most successful groups I've seen begin with a time of fellowship around food. Potlucks work, or church volunteers providing a meal. A separate meeting place for the children to eat will also draw more moms in. (Single moms are worn out! Not having to prepare a meal before coming to a meeting gives incentive to come, and eliminates an excuse for not attending.)

Presenting your vision:

To Your Pastor:

1. Know your local statistic (see page 23 on finding your demographics)
2. Cast vision for this as a local mission field.
3. Your community's next generation is in the balance.
4. Be positive about your church's role in caring for the lost.
5. Let your pastor know you have a team willing to work with you.
6. Be patient if the pastor's timing is not the same as yours. You want to work with your local church and gain support with volunteers to succeed.

SINGLE MOM GROUPS
LEADERSHIP
GUIDELINES

Keep in mind, no leader will be perfect. However, the overall attitude and maturity of the leader will dictate the direction and success of a group. People often believe they are ready for leadership when they have yet to prepare themselves for that role in attitude, training, or self-restoration.

Don't wait for the perfect leader, but be willing to trust the teachable person with leadership.

Suggested Leadership Guidelines

When selecting or accepting a single parent as your your main leader, I suggest they have the following history in your church. (Their 'team' may not have the same experience, because under the right leadership they will grow into it.)

- 2-3 years serving in some capacity (usher, Sunday school teacher/assistant, etc). A serving position that has been observed and supervised by a staff or volunteer leader where they have shown dependability and respect for both supervisors and leaders.
- An attitude that exudes joy, patience, and forgiveness.
- Has shown herself to be rational in her responses under stress.
- Displays self-discipline in their work, home and personal life.
- Is willing to take advice from leadership and is not rebellious in their attitude.

Single parent groups can be great or they can be disastrous. If leadership has not been carefully selected, trained and supervised, they can do more damage than good to single parents and the church.

Option: Choose a healthy couple to have oversight of the group

They may not understand all the issues of being a single parent, but they bring balance to biblical and practical teachings, relational issues, and the overall tone of the group.

A single parent group is not always the right choice

- Groups can separate or isolate single parents from the rest of the congregation. It can leave them feeling discarded, unwanted, or unworthy to participate in the full social and spiritual aspects of the church.
- Groups can force children to remain in single parent social circles when they are in desperate need of observing and learning basic healthy family relationships.
- Without community outreach, there may not be enough single parents to warrant a group in your congregation.
- Developing a single parent ministry to separate the problems these needy families bring to the church will often stunt their spiritual growth and emotional healing.
- *Separation also strips the congregation of an opportunity, and obligation, to reach out to the widows and orphans of their community as the body of Christ.*

Using a website

Many successful groups have their own Facebook page. It's a private page, meaning a person must be accepted to join the group. You can setup administrators for the page who determine who can join the group and also monitor what's being posted. For even more control over the content, you can set it up so that each post must be approved before it's posted.

Groups can post activities, leaders can post helpful articles, mom's pose questions or ask for specific help (ie: moving help, babysitting needs, etc). They will also post when they are going to a movie, the beach, or other activity and ask other moms to join them. Building relationship is the key ingredient to any single mom ministry, and FB is one more tool you can use.

Know your church body and what best fits the needs of your congregation

MOMS & KIDS TRAINING VOLUNTEERS

Working with Children

- Remind volunteers they are not to solve all problems, just have a listening ear and a caring heart.
- Volunteers should meet with the pastor and/or parent to assess the child's needs, abilities, and initial goals before committing to this ministry.
- Train volunteers to recognize when they are in over their heads, i.e: Child's emotional issues are too extensive for them, they are becoming too personally attached to the child, or they do not have the time to give to this ministry.
- Don't overreact; children are not always accurate in their assessment of situations.
- Keep in communication with the parents.
- Never interfere with the parental role. Volunteers should not become a threat to the parent's relationship with the child. **Volunteers are not responsible to give the child a better life, only to help him or her cope with their current situation.**
- Protect privacy. Do not talk about their issues with **anyone**, except the pastoral staff.
- Have regular progress evaluations with parents and/or pastors.

Working with Single Moms

- Be patient, give them time to get their feet on the ground.
- Give them time to *hear* about Christ, *learn* of His promises for their life, and *believe* there is hope for them before quoting scriptures *at* them.
- Teach Godly principles by *example* (forgiveness, trust, kindness, serving, etc).
- Help guide them into making better choices, but do not make their decisions for them.
- Allow them a few failures; changing lifestyles, habits and self-image takes time.
- Celebrate their victories, be understanding in their defeats, and be encouraging for their future.
- Listen, without judgment.
- Give them small goals to attain, this will build their self confidence
- Don't put added pressures on them (ie: do not expect them to work in the nursery.) Give them time to be in God's presence, hear His Word, and be free to respond.
    - After they become stronger, they can begin to serve in church ministries. Give them time to heal, grow, be embraced, and build a relationship with Christ before 'expecting' them or pressuring them to become involved in serving. It's necessary for them to serve, but in the right attitude and timing.
    - Many single moms have lived in isolation as a mode of self preservation so give them time to feel comfortable opening-up and participating.
- Let them believe they are accepted and cared for, by genuine words and actions.

SINGLE MOMS
PITFALLS TO AVOID

Assumptions and judgments

- About their past or present situation
- About their understanding of Christ in their life
- About their future
- About their education, skills or giftings
-

    All single mothers are not alike. Some single moms won't ask for help when they are in desperate need, while others can become overly-dependent by asking for too much help. Some are very mature and responsible, while others are not.

Lack of boundaries for pastors/volunteers

- Never counsel alone (behind closed windowless doors).
- If you must go to the single mother's home for an emergency, never go alone. Take an associate staff member or family member.
- Limit the number of counseling sessions per week (except for real emergencies).
- Limit the number of phone calls you take. Kindly, but honestly, tell them if they are calling too much or expecting too much. Give them boundaries they can follow. Single parents can be very self-absorbed with their problems and may need to be gently reminded of others' needs and family obligations.
- If they are repeatedly given advice they will not follow, it's time to quit counseling them or offering advice until they begin to make choices to change. Simply explain that you will not meet with them again until they have taken step one or the next step in the process of change. It will benefit no one if they want to take up your time and attention, but willfully refuse to change. You cannot make them change, it must be their choice.
- Setup boundaries for financial help. Offer partial scholarships to help reinforce financial responsibility. Exceptions can be made, but paying for everything, all the time, enables poor financial planning and growth on their part.

Unrealistic Timetables and Expectations

- Give them time to heal and recover. Trust must be garnered before change will take place.
- Allow them time to develop a relationship with Jesus by observation of sincere believers, hearing scriptures taught and preached, and by asking questions. Some will fake salvation in order to be accepted by the church.
- Recognize even a small change as a huge step. Some are fighting years of fear, abuse, and out-of-control lifestyles. Change may come slowly, so be patient.
- Allow the children time to learn and observe what Godly love is. Genuine love brings comfort and draws them in. Rigid expectations for their behavior or academic pressures add more stress to their life, resulting in rejection of God and a rebellious child.

> When the unlovable are loved, they have motivation to change
>
> When the hopeless have hope, they begin to set goals
>
> When the bitter are forgiven, they are free to forgive
>
> When the church reflects Christ, lives are changed for ever!

SINGLE MOM OUTREACH IDEAS

Develop programs & mentors for young mothers

MOPS *(Mother's of Pre-schoolers) - or other Mom Groups*

MOPS meetings offer a place where new mothers can ask questions, make friends and glean wisdom from experienced, mature group leaders. MOPS International has resources to help begin a group in your church or community. http://www.mops.org/

1. **Single Moms MOPS** with speakers and studies specifically designed for the single mother.
   - Have evening meetings, rather than daytime, since most single mothers work. Meet during regular mid-week services so children's programs or child care is available (most SM cannot afford child-care fees)
   - Consider an off-site meeting location such a Community Center, library or local coffee shop. This will broaden your outreach into the community.
2. **Military MOPS** works if you live in an area with military bases, you can meet the needs these mothers specifically face.
3. **Teen MOPS** is specifically designed for married or single teen mothers.
   - Let the local high schools and community centers know about your program.
   After a local church Teen MOPS group met for a Christmas celebration, nine young teen mothers from the community accepted Jesus. They heard the real Christmas story for the first time at that meeting!

Mom to Mom groups

Both married and single moms gathering together for fellowship, speakers, questions and answer sessions, panel discussions, and mentoring. All moms, with kids of all ages!

All church 'Helps'

- Annual Turkey (meal) give away at Thanksgiving
- Quarterly oil changes provided by the men of the church
- "Fix it Team" that will help with household, plumbing, or mechanical issues
- "Adopt a family" for Christmas gifts. Bonding and building relationships with a single parent household
- Be creative, be inclusive, be compassionate

Conferences, Retreats, Special Speakers, or Events

Design a one-day or weekend conference planned especially for single mothers.

- Advertise in the community, not just in your church.
- Unite with other churches in your community to reach more mothers.
- Invite a speaker that understands the single mother's needs.
- Choose topics that give practical help and direction.
- Cast the vision to your church.

  o Enlist volunteers to provide child care for the event
  o Enlist the youth group to give free car washes during the meeting (serving the community)
  o Enlist the Men's Ministry to provide an oil change day (announced at the conference)
  o Enlist the Women's Ministry to prepare a breakfast or lunch for the conference
  o Gather new condition clothes or baby supplies to be given away after the event (surprise the moms with these gifts)
  o Solicit door prize gifts that will make the moms feel special

Plan some Women's Ministry meetings with the single mother in mind.

- Choose topics that will draw single moms: loneliness, parenting tips, etc
- Encourage members to invite single moms from their work-place or neighborhood
- Provide child care for guests or single moms (finances often keep single mothers from attending classes or meetings that would benefit them)
- Schedule WM meetings in the evenings or on Saturday's when single mothers are more available, free child care will be a draw!

Promotion of events:
- Advertise outside your church - with permission: Daycare centers, apartment complexes, laundromats, community centers (radio/papers if financially able)
- Use modern design in your promo & titles that peak interest
- Train Workers to recognize visitors - seat them with leadership or social women

SINGLE MOM
TEACHING IDEAS

Ten Basic messages for single moms

1. Abandonment
2. Love
3. Forgiveness
4. Choices
5. Self discipline
6. Child discipline
7. Beyond coping
8. Dare to dream
9. Controlling your finances
10. Relationships

Message suggestions for pastors or class teachers

A   Abandonment

B   Bridge to God

    Blending in

C   Choices

D   Developing Character

E   Energy

F   Faith ~ Fears

G   Giving

H   Hope ~ Healthy relationships

I   Integrity

J   Jump start your life

K   Kicking bad habits

L   Love means what?!

M   Money Management

N   Nothing is impossible for God

O   Opportunities

P   Passion ~ Possibilities

Q   Questions are ok
    Quiet times with God

R   Righteousness means?

S   Solutions
    Salvation means?

T   Trust

U   Understanding Scriptures in
    today's world

V   Vision

W   Who are you?
    Where are you going?
    What are you doing with
    your life?

X   Generation X, Millennials and
    God

Y   Yes to a positive attitude

Z   Zeal for …. (parenting, life etc)

SINGLE MOM GROUP
START-UP RESOURCES

Designing Your Small Group

These are just suggestions to get your own brainstorming sessions going. These have succeeded in other Single Mom startups. Design your group for your women, and how it fits into your church dynamic and vision. Keep in mind, a small group for single moms is not always the answer. Many single moms want to be included with ALL the women of the church, not singled out. However there are great opportunities for discussion and growth in a small group targeting the specific needs of single moms.

Study Book Suggestions

Keep the study to about 8-10 weeks. This is a commitment easier made.

- **The Bible** - Never forget the power of the scripture
  Using only the Bible often takes a more skilled or experienced teacher.
- **"8 Weeks of Love" A Bible Study for Single Moms** by Lois Breit
- **"30 Days of Choices"** A 30 day devotional book by Lois Breit
- **"Psalm 91"** by: Peggy Joyce Ruth (she also has Psalm 91 for Youth)
- **"Breaking Free"** by Beth Moore (can be a lot of homework, break it down to fit your group)
- **"Unglued"** Making wise decisions in the midst of raw emotions by Lysa TerKeurst
- "**Hope & Help for the Single Mom"** by Lori Little (this is a 21 week study, pick and choose topics to fit your group. 21 weeks is too long of a commitment for most.
- **"A Shepherd Looks at Psalm 23"** by Phillip Keller (this is a great look at God's love for us through the eyes of a shepherd). amazon.com $2-3 each book. However, it is not in a Bible study format with questions/answers.
- **"Overwhelmed"** by Jennifer Maggio - Her story from homelessness to a life of faith and victory followed by a Bible study.

Meeting times & Places

This needs to fit your church and SM needs. Successful times: Wednesday nights, Sunday School, or Friday nights with childcare & a meal.
ALWAYS have childcare provided free or for just a couple of dollars (recruit church ministry volunteers).

SINGLE MOMS LOCAL HELP

Practical Local Help

It's very important to research and locate local help for single moms. Being pro-active will save a lot of last minute scrambling when a viable need arises from within your church or your community. Most often single moms will request help in the area of groceries, diapers, housing, utilities. Beyond church help, they may also need, a shelter, affordable professional counseling, and direction for emotional stability.

Food

Google: food shelf or food bank (your city)

Also: keep a list of local food distribution sites and days of operation

Diapers

Google: 'the diaper bank: or "free diapers"

Assistance

www.singlemomassistance.org (enter your state - local cities will be listed)

Housing

Google: housing assistance (your city/county), or www.rentassistance.com

If there are application forms, have some available at your church.

Education

www.helpinghandsforsinglemoms

Many community colleges offer a first class free for those who have never attended, or haven't attended college for a number of years.

Counseling

Have a list of affordable, reputable Christian counseling services available

Other

Connect with your inner city pastors on state and local help available.

Some states have scholarships available for summer Youth & Kids camps.

Some Christian radio stations have benevolence funds.

Be creative in your research, don't limit yourself to government agencies.

DEMOGRAPHIC STUDY
GUIDE

Options - FREE search

factfinder2.census.gov *(site may not be found if you use www. in search)*
   Source: U.S. Census Bureau, 2007-2011 American Community Survey

   TYPE in the name of the city, county or zip code you want to search - GO
      This should send you to the "Community Facts' section on the tool bar
   CHOOSE: (Population on the left column)
      General population and Housing Characteristics in the box on the right
   SCROLL: down to: Household by Type
   (See SAMPLE below to figure your stats)

   SAMPLE: From Detroit, MI
         "Family Households" (families) with children under 18 yrs - 28.6%
            (Note: 9.2% are married couples with children under 18 years of age)
         "Male Householder (no wife present) with children under 18 yrs - 2.8%
         "Female Householder (no husband present) w/children under 18 yrs - 16.6%
         2.8% + 16.6% = 19.4% are Single Parent homes of the 28.6% family
            households with children under 18 years of age
         19.4% divided by 28.6% = **68%** of all households with children under 18
            years of age are single parent homes in this city.
         (It's also Interesting to note on this survey the number of grandparents
         responsible for raising their grandchildren)

UPDATED in 2013 **to accommodate the 2010 census.** The question of single parent
homes was not on the 2010 census questionnaire, so statistics are summarized from the ACS.
There are a number of criteria you can search in these data profiles

Options - Fee Based

www.missioninsite.com - FEE BASED demographic study

This is a site churches can use to find their demographic statistics.

Cost: $150.00* **Executiveinsite** - intended to give an overview analysis of the defined geographic study area. A defined study area can be a school district, a zip code, a county or a custom defined geographic area such as a radius or a user defined polygon. It will give a comprehensive (all of the below) demographic study on the population in your community.

- Under the 'executivesite' demographic section for <u>Mosaic</u> demographics you will find the single parent statistics for your community:

   (sample criteria choices)

   Insite #1: Population, Household Trends 2

   Insite #2: Racial/Ethnic Trends 3

   Insite #3: Age Trends 4

   Insite #4: School Aged Children Trends 6

   Insite #5: Household Income Trends 7

   Insite #6: Households and Children Trends 9

   Insite #7: Marital Status Trends 10

   Insite #8: Adult Educational Attainment 11

   Insite #9: Employment and Occupations 12

   ► Insite #10: Mosaic Household Types 13 ~ This is the SP Section

   Insite #11: Charitable Giving Practices 14

   Insite #12: Religious Practices 15

Cost: $75.00* **Quickinsite** - intended to give more household, family, racial and income trends. It will not be as complete for finding your single parent family statistics.

* *Prices and website guides are subject to change*
* *Some Districts have membership to this website and you can use it for free under their membership.*

CHURCH
PARTICIPATION

Lead Pastors

- **Language:** Be inclusive, change couples to adults. What does family night mean? Can single adults come? They don't know

- **Refuge:** Provide a safe environment from the outside world of harsh treatment and words. Be patient with behavior issues - Jesus can change them, if we love them!

- **Resource:** See Practical Ministry to Moms page 6

- **Recruit:** Volunteers to give rides if needed (even temporarily)

- **Intentional Focus:** ie: bulletin announcements "we're praying for single parents this week" (month), targeted small groups, inclusive promotions

- **Expect:** Be prepared for some mess … Be prepared for some miracles!

Youth Pastors

Group Demographic: If you don't know who your single parent youth are - prepare a simple survey that will not embarrass them. Include other information ie: interests, favorite foods, best day of your life, do you live with both parents, how many brothers and sisters, do your siblings all live with you, favorite sports team, favorite song/group, your worst day … mix it up -but find out who and how many single parent youth attend (do their parents attend church regularly, occasionally, or never?)

Parent Night: Intentionally target parents who don't attend church

- Have snacks or a meal served - Circulate and talk to visiting parents
- Introduce your theme for the year/quarter
- Cast vision for your goals, mission trips, or activities
- Be sure single parents are called and personally invited (use your team)
- Train leaders to recognize & watch for single parents, especially in larger churches
- Have host tables with church moms ready to greet, engage in conversation and welcome single parents (and all newcomers)
- Give out information for other church activities and small groups - Connect them! This may be your only opportunity to make them feel welcome in the church
- Tell them good things about their child (do not discuss problems here)
- Thank them for making the time to come - let them KNOW you care about them

Notes

- Send a note to non-attending single parents (again, use leadership if it's a large group). Express something positive about their child

Call:

- Tell them you are praying for your students families - do they have a need?

Encourage your youth to 'have the back' of new kids at school

- They've possibly moved to a new neighborhood, new school - new students are vulnerable to isolation, and are often targets of ridicule or taunting

- Encourage older teens to tutor younger students (public/open areas)

Seniors

Mentors

- Cooking classes: include how to buy cuts of meat, vegetables, and fruits

- Grandparents: many single parent kids' have no family input

- Prayer warriors: choose families for them to pray for. They may or may not have interaction with the family, but their prayers will impact them.

- Small group leaders: solid Christian couples have a wealth of knowledge, experience, and can set examples of healthy relationships and family life

- Seniors may want to make handmade items for the children - connections!! IMPACTING kids, impacts the parent

Women

Show Compassion

- Choose meeting topics that will interest all women in the church

- Sit with them - engage them in conversation - be a friend

- Do not be threatened by single moms, include them

Men

- **Invest in the Boys**

- Take them fishing, to a ball game, out to eat (always with permission)

- Be an example of a dad, and a caring, strong Christian example of manhood

- Teach them how to fix things (age appropriate)

* Remember: All children's workers must be screened with a legal background check

ABOUT LOIS BREIT
MY STORY
QUALIFICATIONS

Qualifications

- Assemblies of God, U.S. Missionary to Single Moms.

- Raised five children as a single parent: all five know the Lord, and four are in ministry.

- Author: *"8 Weeks of Love"* a Bible study for single mothers; *"30 Days of Choices"* devotional book for single moms; several articles at www.mnbtg.org; and an article "Salvation for the Single Parent Family" which can be viewed at http://www.enrichmentjournal.ag.org/ under the summer 2009 issue.

- Speaker: Conferences, workshops, Women's Ministry events, and Leadership Training sessions (single mom ministry). View www.loisbreit.com for references & more information.

- Ordained minister with the Assemblies of God: over for 25 years with pastoral, administrative, and U.S. Intercultural missions experience.

My Story

Our children were 2, 5, 7, 9 & 11 years of age when my husband left. Like most single parents, I struggled with grief, loneliness, depression, anger & overwhelming responsibility.

It was a long grueling process of healing and recovery, but God was faithful to His Word every step of the way. I had to make many difficult choices, learn new parenting techniques, get back into the work force and balance a very limited budget. I started out hopeless but ended up with a new vision!

My children have grown into responsible, caring adults and some are parents themselves..

I am now a minister, missionary, writer, and conference speaker. Because a church took on the challenges we brought them, our lives and future were changed! They walked us through the worst of times and the best of times, had the patience to let us heal, loved us, and gave us hope.

> My difficult personal experience is now being used to equip churches to help single moms find the same hope, joy, peace, power, and promise that I found through God's people and God's Word.

Made in the USA
Middletown, DE
07 February 2023

24299977R00035